MW01505796

Introduction

This is a story of ideas. It's a story that involves an impossible challenge and an untrained group of strangers. Using the ReVision™ method for innovation, this ragtag committee comes together as an IDEA TEAM.

In this story, you'll learn to look at problems differently. You'll learn how to find and focus on the most important problems and turn every problem into an opportunity – all the while creating clarity and building consensus.

Innovation is a creative solution to a problem. It's all about identifying challenges and objectives. It's about asking the right questions at the right time with the right people. And it's about building ideas, one upon another, until a solution is found. It's also about action. Innovation without action is just an idea. It's action that turns ideas into reality.

Praise for ReVision™

ReVision helped us get to the heart of the issue keeping us from success. The creative insight it provided broke down barriers that we thought were insurmountable. It was tremendous.

Dallas Barnes, Hampton Farms

Our ReVision was highly interactive and engaging. It fostered collaboration and allowed for diverse perspectives to be shared. The process gave us insights to develop a successful plan moving forward.

Vinnie DiSalvo, Cirrus Insight

ReVision provided amazing clarity and a solid framework for charting our future course. Considering our heritage and aspirations, we now have a crystal clear strategy for growth. We could not be more excited.

Paul Kaper, Carlton Industrial Solutions

The biggest takeaway for me is the change in perspective this process gave us and the speed at which we arrived at possible solutions. Instead of only seeing the problems, through the power of "How Might We?" we learned how to see the possibilities. It is a different way of thinking.

Joan Maxwell, Regulator Marine

This is the best process I've ever seen for solving problems while creating something new, different, and distinctive.

John Heeden, Southern Bank

ReVision uncovered more and better questions from what we initially thought were our problems. It expanded our thinking and provided clarity to our situation.

Ben Goetz, EOS Implementer

ReVision changed the way we manage sales and present our brand, and that changed our entire perception of the marketplace. The ReVision results have been astounding.

Jim Skilton, Southern Corrosion

Thanks to the insights and innovation revealed in ReVision, we are successfully telling our story and connecting more meaningfully with our customers and community.

Neill Nelson, Davenport Autopark

ReVision helped us see the operational and marketing changes that were needed to make significant advances toward our goals. We now have a better strategic plan and a clearer picture of how to move forward.

Leslie Isakoff, A Simple Gesture

Acknowledgments

Our thanks to the late Alex Osborne, the father of brainstorming and the author of *Applied Imagination*. In this book, you'll learn the difference between modern brainstorming and the original "idea generator" that Osborne created. We are grateful to Mr. Osborne and his collaborator, Sid Parnes, for their contributions to the creative process.

Thanks also to Min Basadur, author of *Simplexity*. From Min, Skip learned the value of divergent and convergent thinking and that we all have unique gifts and preferences for problem-solving.

We want to give special thanks to Teri Boggess and Skip's wife, Karen, for their tireless proofreading effort, and Skip's youngest daughter, Spencer Grace, for her invaluable editorial feedback.

Start With How Might We?

The ReVision™ Method for Innovation

by Skip Carney

and

Jessica Carney McKnight

©April 2025: ISBN 978-1-7326373-4-4
Reprinted with permission August 2025.

For information about ReVision, The ReVision Gifts InVentory Survey, bulk book orders, How Might We Workshops, or public speaking availability, email: jessica@carneyco.com or visit www.carneyco.com.

Dedication

This book is dedicated to the many clients who have engaged in ReVision to improve their organizations, better serve their customers, and innovate their products and services.

And to my wife Karen and daughters Jessica, Kathryn, and Spencer Grace. You each have unique gifts and make the world a better place in your own special way.

In Memoriam

Skip went to the home for which he was created on July 30, 2025. He lived an amazing life full of light, laughter, and love for those around him, and he did his best to Be the Light. Skip's life and mission statement was a source of inspiration to many. We hope it inspires you.

"I am a source of ideas, inspiration and encouragement. I am a positive-thinking, can-do-attitude person who believes that with God's help, anything is possible. I help people and organizations find their 'WHY?', help them focus on what matters most, and create a path that 'changes their future' with innovative strategies and creative solutions."

Chapter One
The Challenge

The ballroom was filled to capacity. Kelly Harris stood on the dais. He walked three paces to the left, index finger to his lips as if deep in thought. He looked up and then into the eyes of a dozen or more in the audience, one at a time. Suspense hung in the air like a bird on a wire. He took one step forward and said, "So, all that really matters is that you can hit the ball farther than Larry." Laughter rolled through the room. "Thank you. And good night," he said as he moved toward his seat. The audience stood and broke into spontaneous applause. "Thank you, Mr. Harris. That was awesome," the emcee gushed as the assemblage continued its ovation. "Kel will be in the lobby to sign books and answer questions. Remember good ideas, bad ideas, dumb ideas, and old ideas…" He waited, and the entire room shouted in unison, "Are what great ideas have for breakfast!"

Kel was signing books as his fans patiently waited and talked among themselves. "I am eager to share what I learned tonight," said a thirty-something woman. She was holding two copies of *The Creative Committee* and one copy of *The Brainstorm Hack*.

"I can't wait to get back to my missions committee at my church," sighed the gentleman beside her. "Maybe we can actually make some progress this year."

A man stepped to the table. As Kel looked up, he noticed something different about this man. He had no books in his hands. He was well-dressed and fit, about 50, maybe 55, and looked like he had just closed a big deal. "Mr. Harris, I'm Benjamin Landry, and I have a proposition for you."

"Mr. Landry, what can I do for you?"

"One of my employees suggested I come tonight. I heard some of your speech."

"But not all?"

"No, but what I heard was interesting."

"Thank you."

"What does it mean to hit the ball farther than Larry?"

"Oh. Well, that is a simple example of how a solution has to be viewed from the perspective of the intended user or beneficiary. I think you missed that part of my talk."

"Yes, and I confess I also haven't read any of your books."

"Okay."

"As I understand it, you believe everyone is creative."

"That's right. Everyone can be. Everyone can contribute to the creative process. Everyone can be a creative, innovative problem-solver," he said, pausing briefly. "Most importantly, every committee can be creative and productive."

Landry laughed. "I've seen committees kill more ideas than they create."

"I've seen that, too," said Kel. "But, with the right tools, a committee can overcome the hurdles that kill ideas."

"Your tools?"

"Correct."

"You call your method ReVision. What does that mean?"

"In short, we use ReVision for strategic innovation. In my view, innovation is simply a creative solution to a problem. Strategic innovation is a creative solution for a particular purpose. ReVision makes sure we're working on the right problem. It creates clarity, alignment, and focus. And it turns a committee into an IDEA TEAM."

"Really. I heard you say that companies or organizations often fail because they try to solve the *wrong* problem," Landry said, emphasizing the word *wrong*. His eyes were fixed on Kel's, waiting for him to flinch or break into a sweat.

"That's right," Kel said, smiling. "Sometimes, it's because they neglect the needs of their constituents. Sometimes, it's because they refuse to make changes that need to be made." His focus was one hundred percent on Ben Landry. The rest of the room was a blur. "But, more often than not, it's the wrong problem."

"But every problem can be solved, right?" pressed Landry.

"I believe so, yes, sir."

"Mr. Harris, I have a billion-dollar problem. I've had some of the smartest people I know working on it for over a year, and they are stumped."

"Okay."

"I want to give that problem to you."

"I'm listening."

"You can select any of the creative people in this room to work on the project." He put air quotes around the word *creative*.

"And …"

"And I'll give you one million dollars to solve the problem."

"Well …"

"But if you fail, you'll owe me one million dollars."

"Wow. That's interesting."

"Should be easy for an innovator like you. Right?"

"Okay. What's the nature of your problem?"

"Do you accept my challenge, Mr. Harris?"

"I do." Kel looked around the room. It had gotten very quiet. Everyone was leaning in to hear what they were saying. He added, "Yes. I'll accept your challenge. I have just two conditions. First, you need to understand that ReVision is a step-by-step process, and it is important we use it to solve your problem."

"That's why I'm here."

"…and we must follow it to the letter."

"Agreed."

"Great. Second. I want to add one person from your team. Any one of those smart people who have worked on this problem for over a year."

"I thought you might say that, and I agree. That will be my COO, Brandon. He's a bright young guy. I'll make sure he is there." Landry checked his watch. "If that's it, shall we choose your commit-tee?"

"Let's call it a TEAM, Mr. Landry. We'll start with you."

"Of course."

14

"And the next five people in line behind you, assuming they are willing."

"Oh, I think they will be. I'll pay them each twenty-five thousand dollars per week for the next four weeks."

"That should be incentive enough. You'll pay for four weeks even if we solve the problem in one week, right?"

"Yes. Provided you succeed."

"And if we fail?"

"They get nothing. They owe nothing."

"Sounds fair."

"Great. We'll start next week. I'll have my people make all the arrangements — your hotel, meeting space, whatever you need. We'll be in touch."

With that, Benjamin Landry shook Kel's hand, turned, and walked away. The people in line had heard it all. They had watched silently, waiting for a reaction from Kel. He reached for the next book to sign. "What's your name?"

"Katie," she said. "Did he say he would pay me, uh, us, one hundred thousand dollars each to be on your committee?"

"TEAM. Yes, he did. After we solve his problem."

"But I'm not qualified to solve a billion-dollar problem."

"Sure you are. What do you do, Katie?"

"I'm an art teacher."

"Perfect. Can you take some time off next week?"

"We're on break next week, so, yes. Do you think it will take more than a week?"

"Hard to say for sure, but we'll see." Kel pointed to his left. "Katie, I think that young man over there is waiting to get your information."

"Oh, okay." She turned toward the man with the iPad in his hand. The next four people were just as flabbergasted and bewildered as Katie. Cory, the factory supervisor; Heather, the marriage counselor; and John, the retired engineer. The final member of the TEAM was a college student named Tess. She approached Kel's table. "There's no way you want me on this committee." She blushed. "I meant TEAM. I have very little experience or training. I couldn't even buy a book, but one of my professors said I could get class credit if I got your autograph."

"What are you studying, Tess?"

"Business and Philosophy."

"Great combination. Don't worry. You'll do great, Tess. Here's my autograph," Kel smiled as he handed her a signed copy of his book.

Tess turned toward the young man with the iPad. Kel reached for the next book to sign. "Thanks for coming today. What's your name?" The news of the challenge rippled through the room like a wave. Kel continued to sign books and talk with his fans.

The fledgling TEAM stood and watched in silence. Heather was the first to speak. "Did that really happen? Are we really going to be an IDEA TEAM like he says in his books?"

"I wonder what kind of problem we'll be working on," mused Cory as he reached for his phone. "I've got to call my wife. She's not going to believe this."

Katie smiled, "I was planning to read this book next week."

"Me, too," laughed Heather. "I guess we'll get to learn from the master instead."

Lying in his hotel room that night, Kel thought about the challenge. It wasn't the first time someone had thrown down a gauntlet, but it was the first time the stakes were so high. "What could possibly be worth a million bucks?" he said to the ceiling. "I guess we'll find out soon enough. Tomorrow, we start working on the TEAM." He turned off the light and fell asleep.

Chapter Two
The "Committee"

Benjamin Landry was an enigma. He was a self-made billionaire with companies all over the globe, but he had managed to stay out of the spotlight. Even so, there was no lack of information about him. One online search turned up hundreds of pages. He had started a small company in his twenties and turned it into a multi-million-dollar international enterprise before he turned 30. He never married or had children. Apparently, he never had time for that kind of commitment. Not even a pet. He was described as a hard-driving deal-maker. One headline read, "Ben Landry. He loves to win. Hates to lose."

"Enough about Landry. It's time to get to know the committee," Kel said to himself. A package had arrived at his hotel door with a short biography and contact information on each person. The packet included directions to the Landry building downtown and instructions to be there at 8 a.m. Monday. Kel quickly drafted an email.

To: Mr. Benjamin Landry

I would love to visit your offices after we have completed our project. We will work better, though, in a neutral location. My hotel has the perfect space on the second floor. I'll arrange to have it ready for us at 7:30 Monday morning. We'll start with coffee, tea, juice, and a light breakfast with pastries and fruit. At 8, we'll get started.

Respectfully,

Kelly Harris

P.S. I've included a link to a short survey. Please follow that link and complete the survey today. I'll share the results with you Monday.

He clicked the "send" button and proceeded to contact the rest of the team.

To: The ReVision TEAM

Good Evening. Welcome to the adventure. I realize this is something new and different for you. Just remain calm and try to get some rest. You'll learn everything you need to know on Monday, and we'll work together to solve Mr. Landry's problem.

As I mentioned last night in my talk, we all contribute to the problem-solving process. Each one of you is creative in your own way, and you have certain gifts that bring value to the process.

Follow the link below to my Problem-Solving Gifts Inventory Survey. This short survey will help you see and understand the gifts that you bring to the table. I'll explain more when we meet on Monday.

Sincerely,

Kelly Harris

Chapter Three
The Gifts

Ben Landry didn't respond to Kel's email, but at 7:18 on Monday morning, he walked into the Crystal meeting room on the hotel's second floor. It was set up just as Kel had asked: a horseshoe with the open end facing the screen. There were eight chairs around the table with nameplates for each of the six committee members, plus one for Anna and another for Lyndsey, two of Kel's staff members. They had flown in the night before to prepare the room for the day's activities.

"So, this is where the magic happens?" Landry asked wryly.

"We'll see," Kel responded as he turned on his computer. "You're early."

"If you're not early, you're late," Ben said. "Brandon should be here any minute. He knows how I am about …"

"There are Tess and Katie. Good morning, ladies. Who's your friend?"

"Good morning," they responded in concert. They pointed to Brandon and said, "Oh, him? We picked him up in the lobby. Says he belongs here."

"He might be a spy," Katie giggled.

"Hello, Mr. Harris. I'm Brandon. I work with Mr. Landry."

"Glad you're here, Brandon. Help yourself to coffee and pastries," he said, and gestured toward the refreshment table.

"Thank you."

"Here comes John, Cory, and Heather. Good morning. Come in. Make yourselves at home."

It was a little awkward at first, like teenagers at their first school dance. Gradually, each person made their way to the coffee pot to grab a cup of security. Ben Landry was on his phone in the corner. Tess was the first to break the ice.

"Katie, what do you say to a billionaire?"

"Beats me," she said with a shrug.

John stepped closer. "He's no different than the rest of us," he said. "Except for the zeros."

"Zeros?" asked Tess.

"The ones at the end of his bank account," he said, then smiled. "You know, the ones that turn thousands into millions and millions into billions."

"Zeros don't make you happy," said Cory.

"I'd be willing to try," chuckled Heather.

"Me, too," added Tess.

"He's a regular guy," Brandon chimed in. "He's more driven than most folks, and his business savvy is off the charts." Brandon looked toward Landry to ensure he wasn't listening. "Guys, I've known Ben Landry for ten years and worked with him for eight. He's one of the toughest and most compassionate men I know. The softer side doesn't always show, but he has a heart of gold. I've seen it firsthand."

"But look at him," said Heather. "Does he look happy to you? I kinda feel sorry for him."

"He's not unhappy, Heather. He's just really focused on this problem."

Cory changed the subject. "Hey, how do you feel about being on the committee?"

"I get the willies just hearing that word," said John. "My experience with committees is they talk, talk, talk, and rarely act. The only motion that carries is the one to schedule the next meeting."

"I know what he means," whispered Heather. "People are often afraid to commit, to take responsibility."

Cory joined the conversation. "I'm okay with commitment. I'm just not sure we are the right people for the job. I sure don't know how to solve a billion-dollar problem."

Kel interrupted the conversation and asked everyone to take a seat. "I like to start these meetings with a quick introduction. I ask each person to give their name, job title, and the reason they believe they are here."

Heather laughed. "I have no idea why I'm here!" she said.

"Luck of the draw, I think," said Cory.

"Good luck or bad luck?" asked Tess.

Kel laughed. "Okay, you're right. This is a little different. Let's just call it good fortune, and you're all here to help solve a problem for Mr. Landry. So, let's just go with a little bit about yourself personally. Tess, why don't you start?"

"Oh. Okay. I'm Tess. I'm a junior in college. I'm studying business and would like to have my own business one day."

"Great Tess. Now, John. Tell us a little about your background."

"I'm John. I was in manufacturing for 30 years before I retired. I'm an engineer by training, but I spent a lot of my time herding cats, so to speak. I like working with machines. People are a bit challenging. Right now, I volunteer at my church, and I struggle with committees. I'm hoping to learn something that will help there."

"You've come to the right place, John," Kel said.

"I'm Katie. I teach art to high school kids. I love what I do. It has its challenges, but it is also very rewarding. I came to learn more about innovation and creativity."

"I'm Cory. I'm a production manager in a plant that builds parts for the auto industry. I help manage the supply chain, quality control, delivery, people — you name it."

"Heather, here. I'm a counselor. Mostly, I work with couples who are married or are about to be married. I work with all kinds of problems."

Finally, Brandon spoke up. "Hi, folks. I'm Brandon. I guess you know that I am the COO for Mr. Landry. My job is to oversee the operations of his enterprises." He paused. "And to take on any special projects he assigns. Like this one."

"Thanks, Brandon," Kel said and rose to stand. "I'm sure you each spent a little time online learning about Mr. Landry." Heads nodded. "I'm not sure I can add to what you've learned. Mr. Landry, is there anything you would like to share with the Team?"

"Glad you asked. Are you ready to talk about my problem?"

"Almost. But, first, we need to understand each other a little better."

"Well, maybe it will help if we start with this." Landry held up a large manila envelope. "I have here six checks. One for each of you for one hundred thousand dollars," he said, gesturing toward the rest of the team, "and one for Mr. Harris for one million dollars. I'll sign them when my problem is solved." He slid the envelope across the table toward Kel.

"Thank you, Ben. You can hold on to those checks for now. We have a lot of work to do." Regaining control of the room, Kel focused attention on the screen behind him. It displayed the results of the Problem-Solving Gifts Survey. "You each completed the survey over the weekend. Let's talk about what those gifts mean."

"Well, I know what I am. According to your survey, I'm a Mover," exclaimed Landry.

"Yes, you are," said Kelly. "Movers are people of action. They like to get things moving and have little patience with people standing in their way."

He added, "This approach has likely contributed greatly to your success."

"Correct."

"But it has also worked against you at times," Kel added. Landry grunted in response.

"More on that in a moment. Let's go around the table." He gestured to the group. "What is your gift for problem-solving?"

"I'm a Transformer," said Katie.

"Examiner," said Tess. "And Architect," she added. "I've got some of both."

"I think I'm an Examiner, too," Heather said.

"I'm part Architect and part Mover," offered John. "I like to make a plan and then do it."

"I'm a planner, too. I mean, Architect," said Cory.

"What's your gift?" Heather asked Kel.

"I am a Transformer first, Mover second," he said. "I prefer to create ideas and then test them out. Brandon has a preference for ideas, too. Right, Brandon?"

"Yes, sir. According to the survey, I'm a Transformer."

"You transform problems into ideas or potential solutions."

"That's true. Then, I gather the people to vet the ideas and develop and implement a plan."

"What does all this mean?" Landry asked.

"Glad you asked, Ben. You see, 'creativity,' another word for 'problem-solving,' is a process. Each of us approaches problems differently. We each focus on different parts of the process. The Transformer is excellent at transforming problems into ideas or solutions. Ideas come relatively easily for us. We love to brainstorm. We see possibilities where others see problems. The Examiner, on the other hand, prefers to focus on data and information. Examiners are great at research and good at making connections between data points. They like to bring people together and build consensus. They aren't comfortable with moving forward until they know all they can know."

A smile came over John's face. "That explains my church committee," he said. "They must all be Examiners. They can never get enough information." There were chuckles around the table.

"Could be," said Kel. "Architects, on the other hand, are the planners. They can take the ideas and information of the Transformer and Examiner and develop a plan of action. They want to know where we are going before we start. Mr. Landry is Mover first, Architect second."

"That is true," Landry nodded.

Kel said, "But sometimes you allow your Mover instincts to drive decisions. You go with your gut before you have other ideas or all the information. Sometimes, that leads to setbacks. Sometimes disaster."

"Did you read my bio?" asked Landry.

"Just the headlines. Your gift survey told me the rest."

"Interesting. But what does it mean?"

"It means that you each contribute to the problem-solving process," said Kel. "It means that you complement each other. It means you can work as a TEAM more easily now that you understand your gifts. TEAM is an acronym for Transformer, Examiner, Architect, and Mover. You are no longer a committee. You're a team — an IDEA TEAM."

"Just like that?" asked Ben.

"With the right tools," answered Kel. "By the way, IDEA is also an acronym for the four steps of Re-Vision: Identify, Discover, Explore, and Activate. You'll learn about each of those steps as we go through the process."

"So, this is different than brainstorming, I take it?" queried Landry.

Kel laughed. "What you, and most people, call brainstorming, I call corporate torture."

"How's that?"

"You know how it works. The boss gathers a bunch of people in the conference room and announces a problem that needs to be solved, and for the next 30 minutes, the group tries to brainstorm a solution."

"That's how it was at my company," declared John.

"And how did that work?"

"It was brutal, Mr. Harris. Nobody was prepared. All the ideas were actually 'old' ideas. Nothing new. Nothing creative." He paused. "If a truly creative idea came up, it was often shot down as impractical, too expensive, or just plain crazy."

"I've seen that before, too," sighed Landry.

"It happens at my school all the time," exclaimed Katie.

"It's common," said Kel. "That's why I call it corporate torture. Most people struggle with that approach."

"So, there's a better way?"

"Absolutely. ReVision is it." Kel held up a copy of his book, *The Brainstorm Hack*. "It's all in here. What most people don't realize is that when brainstorming was invented back in the 1940s, it was a six-step process—six very intentional steps. What we now call brainstorming was step number four. You know what happens when you skip the first three steps in a process." He let that sink in for a minute.

"Sounds like a recipe for disaster," mused Heather.

"It's like assembling a Christmas toy without directions," said John.

"I get it," said Landry.

"With ReVision, we start by identifying your preference for solving problems, your 'gift.' Next, we get some agreement on some of the issues involved with the problem; then, we search for more, different problems. That exercise alone gets you thinking differently and gets you outside the so-called box. At that point, your brain is actually ready to brainstorm." Kel looked around the room. It seemed they were getting it. "So, who's ready to be an IDEA TEAM?"

"Well, I guess I am."

"Me, too."

"Why not?"

"Great. Let's get started," Kel said, rolling up his sleeves.

Chapter Four
The Method

"I mentioned earlier that creativity, or problem-solving, is a process." Kel was back at the computer. This time, the word IDEA was on the screen.

"So this is just about ideas?" asked Landry.

"No, sir. It's much more than that. As I mentioned, IDEA is an acronym for the entire problem-solving process. It takes us from facts to solutions to action."

"I'm listening."

Kel started again, "I stands for Identify. We have to Identify a problem, the facts related to the problem, and the people who will work through the rest of the process. That's where we are now. We have the TEAM, the people. We'll get to the problem and the facts in a moment."

The room was quiet. Everyone was focused on Kelly. He paced for a moment. "Normally, the TEAM would consist of the five to seven people integral to the organization's future. In this case, it would be the executive team from Mr. Landry's company. We like five to seven because those folks usually represent every aspect of the organization, including operations, marketing, finance, HR, and sales. They all have different perspectives, but they all have one thing in common: They care about the future of the organization and want to solve whatever problems stand in the way of success."

"Makes sense," said Landry.

Kel continued. "In this case, Mr. Landry has challenged us to work on a problem …"

"*Solve* a problem," reminded Landry.

"Correct. Solve a problem. A problem only he and Brandon are familiar with."

"I still don't see how this will work," said Heather. "We have nothing in common."

"I've read his books," John said. "I get the theory. I'm ready to put it into practice."

"We will get to all that shortly," interjected Kel. "For now, let's focus on the process." He moved back to the computer and advanced the deck.

"D stands for Discover. This is the step where we discover new and different problems — often better problems — to solve. You heard me say Friday night that organizations often fail because they are solving the wrong problem. The most creative idea, the smartest strategy, and the best execution will always fail when focused on the wrong problem."

"I don't think I understand," Katie interrupted. "When is the problem, not the 'problem'?"

"Henry Ford understood the concept," answered Kel. "He said, 'If I had asked my future customers what they needed or wanted, they would have said a faster horse.' Ford understood that people actually needed a faster, more comfortable method of transportation. So, he invented the automobile. The horse, as the standard for transportation, became obsolete."

"But …," Tess held up her hand.

"Here's another example: You and your friends want to go out to eat, but you can't agree on where to go until someone says, 'Why don't we just order delivery?' You thought the problem was where to go out to eat, but it was really how to get food and dine together." Kel let that sink in. "Yes, Tess?"

"So, if I want to get my parents to let me stay on campus next summer, the problem could be that I need to make my summer more productive and less expensive?"

"That's right, Tess. It could also be related to 'why' they want you to come home. Do they need your help around the house or in the family business? Maybe you need to get a summer job or take classes to solve one of those problems. Until you know the real problem, you are wasting time looking for a solution. Ask your parents these questions. 'How might I stay on campus next summer? What's stopping me from staying here? Why would you prefer I come home?' Those questions will likely lead to better answers and identify the real problem."

"So, how do we Discover more, better problems?" asked Heather.

"Well, I just demonstrated the key to discovering more problems. First, you ask, 'How might we solve this problem?' Then, 'Why do we want to solve this problem?' And, finally, *What's stopping us from solving this problem?* We will get deeper into those questions in a bit."

Moving on, Kel said, "E is for Explore. After you have found new, different problems to solve, you must Explore new and different ways to solve those problems. This is often the place where new ideas spring up. Discover takes us outside the box. Explore helps us see the box from a different perspective…a different point of view."

"I told you there would be brainstorming," said John.

"You'll love it," Kel said, smiling. "I guarantee it."

"Speaking of guarantees …" Ben pointed to the envelope.

"Yes, Ben. Patience. You, Brandon, and John will like this next part. The A in IDEA stands for Action or Activate. Once you find solutions to your problems, you have to create a plan and then put that plan into Action. When I work with businesses, I separate the problems and the action plan into manageable areas. They include Operations, Finance, Product/Service, HR, Sales, and Marketing. When I work with churches and not-for-profit organizations, we separate the problems by Mission, Ministry, Communications, Purpose, and People."

"My head is spinning," said Tess. "Can we pause for a minute?"

"Absolutely," Kel said. "Let's have lunch. Stretch your legs, get some fresh air, and then we'll stretch your mind. Anna and Lyndsey will lead you to the dining room just down the hall. When we return, we'll review and then jump into Ben's problem."

"At last," said Ben. "I never have been very patient. Now I understand why."

Chapter Five
The Problem

The team was starting to come together. The gifts survey gave them a point of reference. Even though the "problem" was still a mystery, they now knew a little more about how they would be involved in the solution.

"I didn't realize that I always approach problems by gathering information," Heather said to Cory. "But I do. I *am* an Examiner."

"Maybe that's why you became a counselor. It's natural for you."

"How about you, Cory? Is planning a big part of your job?"

"Every day. That's what I do. Managing our production lines is all about making plans, changing plans, and adapting to circumstances. Making more plans." He thought for a second and laughed. "It's my gift."

After lunch, Kel reassembled the group, and when everyone was settled, he started. "You all know why we are here. Mr. Landry has what he calls a billion-dollar problem. I mentioned earlier that we all have something in common. We all have problems we need or want to solve. So, let's quickly go around the table. What's your number one problem? Or why did you come to hear me speak last Friday night? Lyndsey will write your problem on the board."

Katie – "I want to teach my students how to think more creatively, outside the box."

John – "My church committee. I want my committee to stop acting like a committee and get something done."

Cory – "I want my co-workers to learn to solve problems for themselves or at least present some options before bringing me the problem."

Tess – "I need to get my degree and get a good job. The sooner, the better."

Heather – "It's all about my clients. I want to find a better way to help them solve their problems. Maybe, if I can get to the *real* problem, it will be easier."

"Now, we simply turn all those problems into opportunities," Kel announced as Lyndsey wrote the problems on the board.

How might we make committees more productive?

How might we teach students to think creatively?

How might we get factory workers to solve problems on their own?

How might we help Tess graduate soon and get a better job?

How might Heather better help her clients solve their problems?

"Now, Mr. Landry. Let's talk about your problem. You told us that you have had some brilliant people working at it for over a year with no solution." Turning to the group, he said, "He has come to us for a solution." Kel paused for a second. "Ben, in one sentence, please identify your problem."

"Easy," he said as he stood and began to write on the whiteboard. "I want a solution to world hunger and food insecurity." He looked back at the members of his new team and then added, "Within six months." He underlined "within six months" and stepped away from the board. Silence filled the room.

John was the first to speak. "This has nothing to do with your business."

"Correct," said Landry.

"You've been working on this for a year?"

"Right."

Katie spoke up. "Mr. Landry, people have been working on this problem since the beginning of time."

"That's true, Katie."

"How … ?" Tess stood up and then sat down. Her question mark hung in the air.

Kel stepped up. "He did say it was a big problem."

"Yes, I did," Landry said, walking toward Kel. As he handed him the marker, he said, "And now, it's your problem."

"Well, it's our problem, and we'll get started on it in just a few minutes." He glanced at his watch. "Let's regroup in about ten minutes, okay?" The team looked like a small herd of deer caught in the headlights of an eighteen-wheeler. "Folks. Relax. Breathe. Take a break. Clear your head. We'll get started shortly."

The group got up and shuffled toward the door.

"This is gonna take a miracle."

"What the — .?"

"Didn't see that coming."

"Hey, Brandon, I've got a question…."

Kel turned to Ben. "Well, I think you got their attention." He laughed. "I think they need a moment to absorb that idea."

"Mr. Harris, I'm not sure they have a lot of faith in your system."

"The first step is to avoid prejudging the problem or the solution. We have to keep an open mind. Stay open to the possibilities. Every problem can be solved. My mother always said, *Can't never could do nothing.* Not grammatically correct, but it made an impact on me."

"How so?"

"She taught me to eliminate the word 'can't' from my vocabulary and, most importantly, my thinking. She taught me to look at possibilities, not obstacles. I think that's why I like the phrase 'How might we?' It opens the mind to possibilities."

"Mr. Harris, I've built an empire plowing through obstacles. This one, obviously, has me stumped."

"No worries, Ben. When everyone returns, we'll start with 'How might we solve the world hunger problem in the next six months?' By the way, we're on the same team now. Call me Kel."

Landry started toward the door, phone in hand. "I'm not worried, Kel. But I think you should be. The clock's ticking."

The ReVision™ Method for Innovation

Chapter Six
Identify

The TEAM wandered back into the meeting room. One and all, Kel could see the look of defeat on their faces. Brandon was carrying a banker's box full of files. Cory was carrying one as well.

"What's this, gentlemen?" He quizzed.

"Oh, this is just the tip of the iceberg," moaned Brandon. "We have three times this amount of info on my computer. This is the key research we gathered over the past year on the world hunger issue."

"Of course," Kel said, scratching his head. "Just put those on the table over there." He looked around the room. Everyone was getting coffee and a donut. "Okay, let's take a seat and get started."

"What's the point?" asked Heather. "Is there any hope?"

Kel put down the marker and walked to the front of the room. He looked out the window for a full minute. "Good question, Heather. There's an ancient proverb that goes something like this: The journey of a thousand miles begins with a single step." He let that sink in. "We know what the problem is, and we know it's a big problem." Everyone nodded. "The solution is the last step in our journey. We are at the first step. And the very first step is to keep an open mind. If you start by judging, you will miss opportunities to think creatively. Innovation comes when we look at possibilities and ignore anything that looks like an obstacle."

"But some things are just impossible, right?"

"Look around. Think about all the things in your life that you take for granted. Your phone, your car, heating and air conditioning, this building, the chairs you are sitting in. Everything you now know was at one time impossible."

"Oh, I guess you're right," John said, nodding.

Landry spoke up. "When I went into business, everyone from my best friend to my banker told me I would fail. That my idea for business was impossible." He smiled at the group. "A few billion dollars later, you can see how that turned out." Everyone laughed.

Kel picked up the marker and drew a smile and the word 'possibilities' on the whiteboard. "That's more like it. Now, let's get started." He clicked on the first slide in his presentation. It was a quote from Albert Einstein. It read, 'If at first the idea isn't absurd, there is no hope for it.'

"So, we're looking for absurd ideas?" asked Katie.

"That's right, Katie. All the rational, logical, doable answers have already been tried. And we will get to those 'absurd' ideas later. First, we need to gather some facts. So, thinking about this problem, what facts come to mind as important? At this point, all we need are the facts. You don't need to explain them or get into any details. Just the facts."

The TEAM went to work making a list of the key facts and problems associated with world hunger. Lyndsey typed on her laptop as the TEAM called out items like distribution, production, fertilizer, equipment, growing seasons, food costs, access, and protein shortages. When the list reached thirty-five items, Kel paused the group. Lyndsey printed the list on two large sheets of paper. She and Anna pinned them to the corkboard on the wall. "Okay, you each have a set of colored dots at your seat. Bring your dots to the wall and look at these lists. Each of you should choose three items from this list. Choose the top three items that, in your opinion, are the most important facts related to this problem. Don't worry about what anybody else chooses."

With that, the group rose and headed toward the wall with the lists.

"Just three?" asked Katie.

Brandon said, "They're all important. How do we choose?"

"I think that's the challenge," said John. "We have to decide where to focus."

"Well, I know which three I'll pick," Heather chimed in.

"Me, too," added Cory.

Ben Landry picked up his dots. As he approached the wall of lists, he mused. "This is interesting. We tried to tackle all the problems at once." He pulled a dot from his sheet. "Maybe there is something to this ReVision thing."

Chapter Seven
Identify, Part Two

Kel gave the group ten minutes to place their dots. As they settled back into their chairs, he said, "Okay, now that you have all placed your dots, let's talk about the items you didn't select." He waited for a second. The faces before him were filled with questions.

"Yes," he started. "I did say we needed only the facts. So, the only thing I'll say about the items you didn't pick is that, while they still may be important, they didn't merit a dot."

Tess interjected, "That's right. Remember, Brandon wanted to talk about number three, but it didn't get a single dot."

"Exactly," echoed Kel. "So, let's talk about the items you did choose. We'll start at number four. It has three dots. John, Tess, and Katie. I'd like each of you to tell the group why you chose that item. We'll keep going until every dot has been discussed."

For the next forty-five minutes, the team reviewed the list, sharing their perspectives on why they selected the items they picked. Kel explained the value of this step. "We all have different perspectives and experiences, so even though we might have six dots on an item, there could be five or six different reasons for that selection. Talking it through gives us all a deeper understanding and broader perspective on that problem. Any questions?"

John spoke up. "Mr. Harris, there is one item that would have been my fourth dot if I had the option. It turns out that no one put a dot there. Does that mean we forget about item twelve? That doesn't seem right."

"Great question, John." Kel approached the list. "This exercise is all about priorities and focus. Item number twelve is still important, but based on the group's input, we have seven other items that must be addressed first."

Brandon raised his hand. "I can see that now. We spent months trying to solve a problem that was not a top priority. It didn't even merit a discussion."

"At this point," added Kel, "item number twelve isn't a priority. We'll get to it later unless we discover other problems that are even more important."

"Other problems?" asked Landry.

"Ben, we're on a mission to find more problems so we can find more solutions. Lyndsey and Anna will turn these seven problems into opportunities. We'll put those opportunities on the board in what we call the parking lot, and then we'll move into the Discover phase of ReVision and start our Vision Map.

Chapter Eight
How Might We?

While his assistants prepared the opportunity 'parking lot,' Kel explained the magic of 'How might we?'

"I'm sure you've all been in a conversation with a coworker or committee member, and you were working to solve a problem." The group nodded in unison. "While looking at options, you or someone else says, 'Can we do this?' or 'should we try that?' And in a millisecond, the idea is shot down." Another group nod. "The problem is not the idea. The problem isn't the question. It's simply the way the question is asked."

"I don't understand," said Heather. "How do you ask the question differently?"

"If the question can be answered yes or no, it's wrong. It doesn't take any thought to kill a question with a no. It does take thought to solve a problem."

"Okay. How do you get people to think? asked Cory.

"You simply start with 'How might we?' He turned and wrote it on the whiteboard. "When you ask 'How might we?' or 'How might I?,' you trigger the imagination. Your brain goes to work to solve the problem that it previously thought was impossible. 'How might we?' can't be answered with yes or no. It suggests that there is a way to solve the problem. It's probably a way that you haven't thought about before. 'How might we?' IS the brainstorm hack. It's the get-out-of-jail card for people who struggle with traditional brainstorming. For those of you who are process-oriented or thrive on order, 'How might we?' engages your imagination to create solutions in ways your rational brain would normally reject. We will use 'How might we?' in conjunction with two other questions to unlock better problems and better solutions."

Kel walked to the big screen. It now had seven digital sticky notes that Lyndsey had created while he was talking. "You all identified 'distribution' as a major part of our world hunger problem. Lyndsey has turned that into 'How might we distribute food to those who need it?' Likewise, you identified 'nutrition' as a big problem. That problem is now an opportunity called 'How might we ensure the food people eat is healthy and nutritious?' Does everyone understand how that works now?"

"So far, so good," said Landry.

"Great. So, from now on, always start your problems with 'How might we?' instead of 'Can we, should we, could we?' Let's find some more problems to turn into opportunities."

Chapter Nine
Why?

"Okay, TEAM, we've identified some of the challenges with solving the world hunger problem in six months. Let's look at the challenge from a different perspective by asking *Why?*"

"Why do we ask why?" chuckled Katie.

"Asking *Why* helps identify and clarify our objectives while uncovering problems that might be just as important as the initial question."

"Oh. I get it," said Katie. "Where do we start?"

"Take your notepads and pens and write down your number one reason why we want to solve the world hunger problem in six months." Don't share your answer with anyone else just yet. Keep it simple. It can be a word or two or a sentence. Just take a moment to jot it down." Kel took a sip from his water bottle and waited until it appeared everyone had finished writing. "Okay, now think about that other answer you considered. What's the second reason we want to solve the world hunger problem within six months?" He smiled for a second. "By the way, because I want to get a hundred grand from Ben Landry is not an acceptable answer." He winked, "That can be your third answer."

Within a few minutes, all the pens were down, and Kel was back at the front of the room. He started with Tess and went around the room asking the question, "Why do we want to solve the world hunger problem within six months?" Anna typed the answers, and they appeared on the big screen.

Tess said, "World peace." She smiled. "I think people fight when they are hungry and insecure."

Anna listened, typed, and turned each of the team's problems into 'How might we?' statements. When it came to Ben Landry, he was staring at his notepad with a pained look on his face.

"Ben. It's to you now."

Landry stood up slowly. His countenance had changed. For the first time, he seemed vulnerable.

Even Brandon leaned in, curious about what was to come next. He started slowly, "I didn't want to get into this, but it appears transparency and the truth are important to this process. So when you ask, 'Why do I want to solve this problem within six months,' the answer is simply that I have only six months to live, and I want to do something significant before I die." He sat down. There was silence in the room. The TEAM looked back and forth at each other. Kel took a step back. The only sound was the clicking of the keys as Anna typed, *How might Ben Landry do something significant before he dies?* She looked up at Kel, and a tear trailed down her cheek.

The group sat silent and motionless for a small eternity until Tess got up and walked to Landry. He stood, and she wrapped her arms around him. He welcomed the embrace. As she pulled away, she saw a tear stain on his suit. "I'm sorry, Mr. Landry, I, uh…"

"It's okay, Tess." He handed her his handkerchief. "I've made my peace with the idea that I won't be here forever. I just want to leave something behind that will last forever."

Anna started typing again. The words appeared on the big screen. 'How might Mr. Landry leave something behind that will last forever?'

"Does anything last forever?" asked Katie.

"Well, solving hunger would be something big," said John. "Forever? I don't know."

Kel moved back to the whiteboard. He wrote 'Why?' at the top of the board and 'What's Stopping Us?' at the bottom. "Ladies and gents, this would probably be a good time for a pause." As the group filed out of the room, he turned to Ben. "Are you okay?"

"Sure. Sorry to drop the bomb that way. I think I shook up your folks a little."

"They just need a minute to adjust their thinking." Ben sat down. "Ben, are you sure you are all right? You look a little flushed. Let me get you some water." He turned to get a bottle of water from the fridge. When he turned back, Ben Landry was slumped over in his chair, unconscious.

Chapter Ten
What's Stopping Us?

Kel left the information desk at the hospital and took the elevator to the sixth floor, room 611. It had been two weeks since Ben Landry's "episode," and this was the first day he was allowed to see visitors. Kel gently knocked at the door. He could hear Brandon say, "Are you expecting someone, sir?" And he heard Landry's response.

"I expect that will be Kelly Harris. Come on in, Kel."

Landry was sitting up in his bed, an IV in one arm and an oxygen cannula in his nose. "It's not as bad as it looks, Kel. Come in. Have a seat."

"Well, it looks pretty bad."

"Okay. Maybe it isn't good, but for the moment, I'm okay. Brandon here says you've been busy."

"That's true. We have." Kel took a seat by the window. "Has he filled you in on your TEAM?"

Brandon stood up. "No sir, I saved that report for you. I need to make a couple of calls, so I'll leave you to it." He shook Kel's hand and turned to go. "I'll be back."

"Ben, what's the word from your doctors?"

"Well, it turns out they were a little optimistic when they gave me my original expiration date."

"So, it's less than six months, I take it."

"Considerably." The heart monitor beeped for a couple of seconds. "Hey, ignore that thing. It goes off every five minutes for no apparent reason." He refocused on Kel. "I was surprised when Brandon said you continued to work on my problem. You didn't have to."

"We did pause for a day. It was pretty traumatic when they hauled you off in an ambulance, but the whole group agreed to reconvene the next day and continue your ReVision."

"Well, what happened while I was unavoidably detained?" He chuckled, and then he coughed.

"Sorry, apparently, laughter is not the best medicine for me."

"It's okay. Just relax, and I'll walk you through the Vision Map on my computer." He pulled out his laptop and connected it to the TV hanging on the wall. "Ben, you remember we had identified several challenges to the hunger issue, and by asking *Why*, we discovered some new issues, specifically your desire to do something significant before you — "

"I do remember."

"In addition to asking *Why*, we also discovered more challenges by asking *What's stopping us?*" He had the Vision Map on the screen. "When we ask *What's stopping us from solving the world hunger issue?* we get a number of different answers. We turned each of those answers into opportunities by adding 'How might we?' Each opportunity — I call each one a 'How might we?' — each one is written on a digital sticky note like you see here and placed on the Vision Map. For instance, 'How might we make food more affordable?' plus 'How might we create more awareness about food insecurity?' and *How*

might we get more people involved in solving this problem?"
He turned to Landry. "Make sense?"

"Sure. How do you decide where to put the sticky note on the map?"

"Good question. The *Why* answers go above. The *What's stopping* answers go below."

"So, the *Why* answers are more strategic. The *What's stopping* answers are tactical."

"Right. As we build the map, the further up we go, the closer we get to your ultimate mission — closer to heaven."

"And as you go down? Hell?"

"Ha! To some, maybe. Down takes you into the weeds — the smaller challenges that ultimately support the bigger vision."

Ben was studying the map. "Okay. So, when you asked *Why do we want to solve the world hunger issue?* one of the answers was, 'So people would be healthier.' When you asked *Why* to that question, you got 'so people would live longer.' And when you asked, *What's stopping people from living longer?* you added sticky notes for *How might we cure cancer, How might we end wars?*, and *How might we reduce obesity?*

He rubbed his temple with his fingers. "My head hurts. Did you answer all those questions?"

"We answered the most important questions. But, first, we had to find more problems."

"Great. More problems. Okay."

"As you can see, the TEAM quickly recognized that hunger was not the only challenge."

"It was the only challenge that mattered to me," injected Landry.

"Well, there is this other one. The last challenge Anna typed before you collapsed. It reads, "How might Ben Landry do something significant— something that will last—before he dies? We dedicated most of our time to that challenge."

"And why did you do that?"

"I'm sure you recall our first conversation about solving the right problem."

"I do. You said that most organizations waste a lot of time and resources chasing the wrong problem."

"World hunger is a problem, but it was not your only problem. Time was also your problem," said Kel.

"Oh. Right." He adjusted the cannula. "I guess the bet is off if we don't have six months."

"No, sir. We just have a different problem to solve. A different challenge."

"Okay. I guess I did say we would follow your method." He scratched his head. "So, what did you find?"

"More problems. More opportunities." He pointed to the screen. "Look. Brandon told us you have more than one million employees worldwide. When we asked *what's stopping us from doing something significant, something world-changing while you are alive?*, one of the answers became a new opportunity: *How might we use your workforce to change the world?*"

Kel stood up as Brandon returned.

Ben looked at the monitor for a minute.

"You know, if you count spouses and children, we're connected to three or four million people. And if you count all their connections, friends, and social media contacts, you're talking hundreds of millions."

Brandon added, "In fourteen countries, Mr. Landry. If you include our suppliers and customers, we have connections into millions more homes and businesses and dozens more countries."

"Of course. And I never thought of that," Landry said.

"You also have political influence, Ben. We created a challenge called *How might we use your political and business connections to change the world?* We liked that one."

"Okay. I can see some possibilities there."

"We spent two days asking *Why?, What's stopping?,* and *How Might We?* until we had a complete Vision Map. There were more than two hundred 'How might we?' opportunities on this map." Pointing to the screen, he said, "You'll notice this group of notes is related to your mission and vision to do something significant. This group is all about the hunger issue. This group involves your employees. This group is about resources and connections. This group is more aspirational. This group is more tactical."

"Got it. How do you decide where to start?"

"We let the team decide. Just as we did before, we asked each team member to select the four or five

'How might we?' challenges in each area to focus on. Once that was done, each person explained why they chose each one. In the end, there were three big challenges that the group all agreed were the most important to take to the next level." Kel's phone rang. As he reached for it, he said, "And I'll tell you all about that in just a moment. Excuse me." He left the room.

"Brandon, what do you think?" asked Landry.

"I like it. The next phase is what he calls Explore. It's kind of like brainstorming but more fun. The TEAM has some excellent ideas. They are creative, interesting, new — "

"New ideas? Really?"

"Really." He nodded. "I can't wait to share them with you."

Chapter Eleven
Explore

Kel returned in two minutes, but he was not alone this time. "That call was from a friend here in the hospital. I got permission to invite a few friends who wanted to see you." Each TEAM member entered the room individually, gathering around Ben Landry's bed. Tess was the last to come in. She grabbed Ben's hand and squeezed it. "You're looking good, Mr. Landry."

"Liar," he said.

Laughter filled the room. Ben held back a cough. He wiped a tear from his eye.

"I understand you folks have been busy," he said.

"Yes, sir." And for the next few minutes, they made small talk: the news he had missed, the changing weather, and their families. Then, Kel turned their attention back to the Vision Map.

"Mr. Landry has seen the map. Before I came to get you, I explained how you decided to focus on three main challenges to Explore. John, why don't you explain the Explore process?"

"Sure thing. We started with, *How might Mr. Landry do something significant or world-changing?* Before we started to Explore new ideas, Mr. Harris gave us some simple rules: No one was allowed to say 'but' or 'can't.' Every idea has to start with *How might we?* and every idea, even bad ideas, can lead to a great idea, so every idea goes on the list."

Heather chimed in. "Then we looked at the problem from different angles, including the opposite approach, in color and black and white. We looked at what others had considered significant achievements in history. Could we build on those ideas? If others had gone one way, could we go another?"

"Zig instead of zag," added Katie. "Or was it zag instead of zig?"

Cory injected, "Tess suggested you adopt a thousand children."

"Since you don't have family," Tess added. "It was a crazy idea. I admit."

"Yes, but that led us to think about your employees as family and what that would look like if you adopted them," Cory said.

"What would that look like?" quizzed Landry.

John piped up. "We had at least a dozen great ideas. You could provide college tuition to employees and their children; you could pay for weddings; you could provide daycare and free telehealth services."

Tess jumped in, "But the idea we liked best was a Dream Reacher."

"What's that?" asked Landry.

"So, you've got like a million employees, right?"

"Right."

"Okay. That's at least one million dreams. Some dream of homeownership; for some, it's a new car or a boat. Some want to save for retirement or start a small business. Some want to be inventors. Some want to live in a safer neighborhood. You could provide the teaching and encouragement to help your people reach their dreams."

"Dream Reacher. Interesting." Landry scribbled a note on a legal pad by his bed. "So, if I help them achieve their dreams, they'll be happier, maybe even healthier. More productive, better employees."

"It's a win-win!" exclaimed Tess.

"And, did you work on the hunger problem?"

Cory stepped up. "We did. My favorite idea was when Brandon said, *How might we get all of Mr. Landry's employees involved in solving the world hunger problem?* That led to a whole series of new ideas."

"And?"

"Since we had already established that awareness of the hunger issue was a problem, we also know from our research that awareness of how to help was also a big problem," Brandon paused. "I think it was John who said, *How might we get millions of people to donate food each month to a local food pantry or food bank?*"

John jumped in. "It was one of the many projects my church tried to get involved in," he said with a grimace. "Tried but failed. We had willing donors but no consistent way to deliver the food. And then

Katie asked, *How might we use a delivery service to pick up the food and take it to the pantry?* That was genius."

"That's when the plan started to come together," Brandon, excited now, added. "We can start a program where people contribute fifteen dollars' worth of food every month or so. They notify the delivery service that the bag of groceries will be on their front porch. The service picks up the bags and takes the goods to the church pantry. Then anyone in need shops the pantry, paying whatever they can afford."

Landry held up his hand. "Wait. Churches have been operating food pantries for decades. What makes this program different?"

"You do, sir." Brandon smiled so big he broke into a laugh. "The delivery service is the United States Postal Service." He paused for effect. Before Landry could ask, he continued. "We contacted the President—yes, the President of the United States —and asked if we could pay the Posta Service two dollars per bag for pickup and delivery."

"I'll bet he loved that idea."

"He did. So, we challenged our IT department — your IT department — to create an app that would make it easy for anyone to schedule a pickup. It would automatically put their address into the mail carrier's route, and the carrier would pick it up the next day."

"And?"

"The app is finished. We're testing it now." Brandon smiled. "By the way, you're buying new tablets for every mail carrier in America. I hope that's okay."

"Fantastic!" Landry's wheels were turning. "Now, how ..."

Brandon injected, "How do we get the churches involved? Easy. The President sees this as a major initiative that can actually balance the Postal Service budget. When you give the word, he'll call a press conference to announce the program and encourage every church to work with the other churches in their community to create a pantry or food bank and promote the idea to their members."

"Amazing."

"Once this gets going, we will go international," Brandon was glowing now. "Mr. Landry, we have found an organization that builds churches in Third World countries. They've built more than forty thousand churches for less than fifteen thousand dollars each. And they don't just build the buildings. They help guide the pastors and congregants. These churches are integral to their communities." He paused for a moment. "And you've just committed up to ten million dollars a year to build about six hundred and fifty churches yearly. And we will ask all your friends to join the program."

"All my 'rich' friends, right?"

"Yes, sir. And there's more. We have a plan to help people grow more of their own food. We are working with an international civic organization to dig wells and teach fundamental agricultural principles. This is just the beginning."

"Wow. You've made more progress in two weeks than we made in a year. Great job, TEAM. Great job." He looked out the window as he wiped a tear from his cheek.

Kel intervened. "Hey, guys! I think Mr. Landry has heard enough for today. I promised the nurse we wouldn't overstay our welcome."

Ben Landry had a look of peace. A tired look. But peace nonetheless. "Thank you all. I'm, frankly, a little overwhelmed. Thank you."

Chapter Twelve
Action

Landry motioned to Kel to hang back as the group was leaving the room. "So, what's next?"

Kel closed the door. "After Explore, we move into Action, and thanks to your resources and connections, we've been able to move at extraordinary speed."

"I guess it helps that I'm nearly out of runway," he smiled.

"Well, there is a sense of urgency. And you have a lot of friends who care." He put a hand on Landry's shoulder. "We haven't solved the problem yet, but we're off to a pretty good start."

"That's an understatement, Kel. People have been working on this for decades, perhaps centuries. Mostly, they've thrown money at the problem. You actually found a way to throw people at the problem."

"People are always the best solution, Ben."

"Speaking of which. Do you still have that envelope I gave you?"

"The one with the checks?"

"Yes. Of course."

"You can cash the checks now. You've earned it."

"Well, I've already talked to the TEAM about it. They all want to put the money toward the cause."

"Seriously?"

"Yes, sir. Katie wants to create a program to teach young children about hunger and nutrition. Heather will use her counseling skills to set up an online portal to help your employees reach their dreams. John wants to build fifty churches in Africa. He was there two years ago on a mission trip. Cory has a …"

"I get the idea. And you? What will you do with a million dollars?"

"I'm going to give it back to you."

"Why?"

"We didn't finish."

"I disagree. Your method did prove that I was trying to solve the wrong problem, and your TEAM created some brilliant ideas to solve the 'six-month' problem." He chuckled. "The hunger challenge was important, but my real goal was to do something significant before I die. Something more than accumulating a big pile of cash. You've done that. Sure, there's more work to do, but I can see where this is going, and I'm satisfied that this is something that will last. Might even have an EROI."

"EROI? What's that?"

"You know, Kel. An eternal return on investment."

"I like that." Kel nodded and smiled as he took the check from his coat pocket and tore it in two. "And I believe you're right."

He stood.

"Kel, one more thing before you go."

"Yes?"

"This has been on my mind. What does it mean to hit the ball farther than Larry?"

Kel laughed. "Oh, that." He took a step toward Ben. "It was my first client, the company that invented a better way to sell golf equipment. It was a combination of video and computers that would analyze a golfer's swing to help them improve their game. They were having trouble getting traction, and they called me to help. They told me all about the technical aspects, computer algorithms, and the protocol for recommending the correct shaft, grip, and head. All the stuff engineers like to talk about. I put them through ReVision to pinpoint their problems and define their *Why*. At the end of the day, it wasn't about the equipment, stance, swing, or detailed computer analysis. It was about hitting the ball —"

Ben finished the sentence. "Let me guess: — farther than Larry."

"That's it. Larry is that one guy in every foursome who may not be the best golfer, but he always hits the ball farther than everyone else. He's the guy everyone wants to beat. When they started selling that message, they started selling more equipment."

"I know that Larry guy."

"I think you are that guy, Ben. But I don't know that anyone will hit the ball farther than you this time."

"We'll see. We'll see." There was a look of satisfaction on his face. With a touch of sadness. "I wish we had time to do more, Kel."

"Me, too, Ben. Me, too." He shook Ben's hand and headed toward the door. Turning, he winked and said, "How might we? I'll think about that."

The end.

A Message From the Authors

Whether you are working to solve world hunger, planning a family vacation, or developing the next big thing, ReVision is a tool you can use to think different, innovate, and move forward.

Remember, everything you know now was at one time impossible. When you bring your TEAM together and change their thinking with ReVision, every problem can be solved, and every bridge can be crossed.

So, next time you run into a problem, ask, *How might we?* You might be amazed at the answer.

Skip Carney and Jessica Carney McKnight

For information about ReVision, The ReVision Problem-Solving Gifts Inventory Survey, bulk book orders, How Might We Workshops, or public speaking availability, email jessica@carneyco.com or visit www.carneyco.com.

For more info on topics discussed in this book:
For food insecurity, visit www.asimplegesture.com.
For international church development, www.icm.org.
For third-world development, visit www.rotary.org.
For the Dream Reacher concept, The Dream Manager by Matthew Kelly.

Also by Skip Carney

The Greatest Church in the World, A Lamp on a Hill
The story of a young pastor who is about to give up the ministry. He stumbles into a small, out-of-the-way church where he learns the principles that make a church a great church.

The Greatest Disciple in the World, Be the Light
This is the story of a young girl who has lost her mother and her faith. She is mad at the world in general and God in particular. Asking questions, she learns what it means to be a disciple.

Both books are available at www.amazon.com.

Illumination, A Study Guide for the Greatest Church in the World.
This workbook is designed to help church members and leaders identify and remedy the challenges they face. It is available at no cost in PDF format. If you would like a copy, email jessica@carneyco.-com. To order a printed copy, visit:
www.foundationforchristianeducation.com.

17051587R00049